THE IMPRESSIONABLE YEARS

Darlene Landon-Ahdieh

PublishAmerica
Baltimore

ISBN: 1-60441-301-8
PUBLISHED BY PUBLISHAMERICA, LLLP
www.publishamerica.com
Baltimore

Printed in the United States of America

For Mom
And my three sisters.

May we always be happy.
We reflect over the years
We know why we are happy.
Love, love, love.

Through the Eyes of a Child

The year was 1957, I was 13 years old, and I will never forget the special way I felt each time we made this trip. Daddy and I went around the sharp curve in the road that followed the river going west toward home. The car hugged the curve, and I gripped the soft, velvety upholstered seat with both hands so I wouldn't lean over and distract the driver I so dearly admired. As we drove out of town, the car windows were rolled completely down and the air floating in was beginning to have the unmistakable aroma of finally entering the rural area of Anderson, Indiana.

The old, four-door Buick that Daddy was driving headed home as though it had a mind of its own. And I always imagined that Daddy could drive this route blindfolded, because he drove this familiar path so often.

Sometimes when he couldn't get away from work to pick us up, he would send one of his employees to drive us home. Eddie would chauffer us. Eddie was a real character that no one—absolutely no one—could forget once they had met him. He was an older man. He wore glasses with lenses as thick as the bottom of a Coke bottle. He was very kind and treated us as though we belonged to him. He was married, but had no children of his own. And as the years went by, he and his wife found a special place in their heart for my youngest sister.

Daddy was our soul means of transportation for several years. Mom did not drive a car until much later in her life. So after my oldest sister DeAnna got her driver's license our transportation problems improved tremendously. Regardless of who was driving, when we traveled as a family, the old Buick was usually loaded—with kids.

As we headed out of town, our real trek home began at the big yellow board triangle on the curve. This ultimately directed drivers to turn left into the area of newly built homes called Edgewood or follow the road along the river, which led west and directly into the country or "booneys," as we called it. Of course, we headed out to the booneys. We passed fields of wheat and corn. We passed empty pastures and acres of trees. There were only four or five houses on the half-mile stretch until we reached our house.

His, Hers, and Ours

There were five of us kids living in our home on West Eighth Street Road. I was the second oldest in the family. Well, let me retract that statement and clarify it. Actually there were seven kids in our family. Daddy had two sons by his first wife. David and Jimmie lived in southern Indiana with their mother. Then there was my older sister, DeAnna, and me. We were Mom's by an earlier marriage; and Jerry, Janie, and Jacque, were Mom and Daddy's biological children. I grew up with an extended family, as it is referred to now, with seven children—all of us belonging to Mom or Daddy biologically. After we grew up and understood the situation, we lovingly referred to the offspring of our parents as his, hers, and ours.

We were a very close family growing up. There was a lot of love in our family. Except for the five years in age between DeAnna and me, there were about two and a half years between the rest of us in age.

Until I was thirteen, I had no idea the three younger kids were my stepsiblings. Or that I had two half brothers living in Evansville, Indiana.

DeAnna knew. Even though I knew Daddy drove to southern Indiana often. And even though I knew he left very early on Christmas Eve but returned late in the night to be home for our Christmas morning. And even though DeAnna and I went to visit our grandparents without any of the other kids, I still did not realize the family situation.

DeAnna said later that I should have figured it out for myself. I guess I just didn't put two and two together. In fact, the day I found out we were not biological sisters and brothers was probably the most unforeseen moment in my entire life.

Reality Sets In

I was thirteen years old and was sitting in English class at Madison Heights Junior and Senior High School. The school secretary came in the room and handed my teacher a pink slip of paper. The teacher called me up to her desk and told me to report to the office. My father was coming to pick me up. Of course, I did exactly as I was told.

I went to my locker and got my books and jacket and went to the office to wait for Daddy to pick me up.

Daddy pulled up to the front entrance of the school. I went out and climbed into the lumber truck. Daddy only said, "Hi Susie." I acknowledged his greeting, but did not ask any questions as to why I was leaving school—without the other kids.

Daddy drove to downtown Anderson and we went into the Anderson Bank Building. Without any conversation, we rode the elevator to the third floor and proceeded to go into an office; on the door I remember reading Attorney At Law in bold, black letters. The office was small, crowded, and very untidy. The woman sitting behind the desk was dressed in a navy blue suit and a white blouse with ruffles. She looked very intimidating to me. I was very nervous as I slowly sat down in a burgundy leather chair. Daddy sat down in a chair beside me. He introduced me to the lady. She spoke to me but seemed very unfriendly. She was very professional but appeared to be strictly business. She immediately looked directly at me and asked me if I liked living with Jimmie. I quickly looked at Daddy for reassurance that I was really supposed to be in this office answering such a silly question.

He sat motionless—looking at the floor—never making eye contact with me.

Of course I answered yes, still not knowing exactly why she was even asking me this question. The look on my face must have made her realize that I had no idea what I was doing there in the first place. She asked Daddy to leave the office a few minutes so that we could talk privately. He did.

She then proceeded to tell me that Daddy, or Jimmie as she referred to him, was planning to adopt me and my older sister DeAnna. Again, feeling somewhat dumbfounded, I listened as she told me that Jimmie was not my biological father and that Mom had been married to my real father but had divorced several years ago. It was now necessary to legally adopt both of us girls because DeAnna was planning on being married soon. We had both been using Daddy's last name and we needed to correct the situation before she could get married.

I listened very patiently to the attorney as she explained our family situation. I didn't question or comment—I guess I just didn't know what to say or think. She summoned Daddy back into her office, we signed our names to some papers, and the matter was never mentioned again until much, much later in my life.

Be Seein' You — Jimmie

While we were growing up, Daddy owned and operated a lumber yard in Anderson, Indiana. It was called ABC Lumber and Millwork and was located on the corner of 4th and Meridian Streets. The slogan for the lumberyard "Be Seein' You—Jimmie" seemed to invite everyone to stop in for all their lumber and building needs. And they did just that. Everyone in Anderson and several surrounding towns knew Daddy and did business with him when they needed lumber supplies.

Daddy had fifty park benches made with his slogan printed on each bench. The benches were placed at bus stops around the city of Anderson. I know the advertising on the benches was one reason Daddy placed them at bus stops. But I like to think it was just another way that Daddy showed his kindness and caring for others. Everyone rode the bus in those days. Everyone worked long and hard hours. Everyone was exhausted as they waited for the bus to take them home each evening—daddy knew that too.

Today, one of the original benches proudly has its own special place in my sister Jacque's house rekindling fond memories of Daddy's successful business. Everyone who ever heard of Jimmie Jaquess knew him to be an honest, compassionate, and fair man. He had a very strong strength of character. His word was everything, and he followed this principle throughout his life.

As my Uncle Bobby tells the story, in the old days when a freight train loaded with lumber would ramble into town, Daddy had three days to unload it. He would round up Uncle Bobby, Uncle Bobby's dad, and other friends to pitch in and help unload the train cars. Without discussing a stipend, Daddy's friends would unload the lumber in one long, tiring day. Even though money was never mentioned, these men were treated more than fairly whenever they needed any building materials. Daddy never forgot that they had been there for him.

What You Get for a Nickel

Occasionally, while in my teenage years, if I had something important to do in town, I would walk down to the lumberyard to catch a ride home with Daddy.

As I walked into the lumberyard office, an enormous feeling of pride overwhelmed me. Just the thought that my daddy owned this big place was so hard for me to believe.

And did I ever feel special when Daddy reached into an old rusty, bright blue, Maxwell House Coffee can under the counter and handed me a nickel for a bottle of Coke. I felt as though I owned the world as I put the nickel in the slot and opened the big red Coke chest. I carefully chose my special bottle, grabbed the neck of it, and slid it down the long metal row. I listened to the loud clanging of glass bottles as I pulled my bottle up and out of the machine.

As I walked through the mill drinking my Coke, the sound of the saws humming and the loud banging of the hammers pounding away just reinforced the pride that had washed over me only minutes before. The loud chatter of voices, the smell of fresh sawdust, and the creaking of the old wood floor never changed over the years as I revisited the lumberyard and hung around waiting for Daddy to take me home.

A House with Pitfalls

In 1947, Daddy found the perfect house in which to raise his family. The old house was just that: an old house. But soon it was ours, we were happy together, and we loved everything the old house had to offer.

As the story goes told by my aunts and uncles, Mom fought Daddy "tooth and nail" when he decided to purchase the old house. Mom said, "It was way out in the country. It had a steep, rugged hill for a yard, no inside running water, an outhouse, and it was situated on a road that the cars traveled too darn fast on." Those were her only reasons for not wanting to purchase the house. Of course, Daddy promised with all his heart he would remodel and update the house immediately after moving in.

I can understand—daddy's "immediately" was just not as "immediately" as Mom thought it should have been. As a matter of fact, it ended up being almost twenty years until the remodeling was completed.

Daddy never got in a hurry about anything. He took his time, but everything he did was perfect. He was a perfectionist as well as a very talented man with many woodworking skills that would surpass any carpenter anywhere.

Buckets of Water

Our old house did not have indoor plumbing. We had an outhouse just east of the driveway under an old walnut tree. And our house did not have running water. We had a well behind the house, and our pump was down in the basement.

Mom, Daddy, and DeAnna (because she was the oldest) had to carry water buckets up old rickety, crooked, wooden stairs from the dark, smelly, dirt floor basement. By the time they balanced themselves on the steps and juggled the bucket, they were sopping wet from the sloshing cold water.

This water was the coldest, clearest, and best tasting water ever. In fact, some of my aunts and uncles used to come out to our house and take some of our water home in jugs to be used for drinking because they loved it so much. And it tasted so much better than city water.

We had a white enamel two-gallon bucket with bright red trim around the top. Big chips of enamel were missing at different places on the bucket, probably from getting clunked against the steps as it was carried up from the basement. This bucket was sitting on the kitchen cabinet to be used for drinking water. We kept a tin shiny dipper with a long handle hanging on the side of the bucket.

As I got older, stronger, and big enough to carry heavy buckets of cold water up the old stairs, I became very adept at getting the last drop of the drinking water out of the bucket and returning the dipper to its hanging position without making an absolute sound. Always remembering Daddy's rule: If you emptied the bucket—you had to fill it up! And company wasn't excluded from this rule.

A Kitchen Sink

The plumbing in the kitchen was the first major improvement of the house. Mom was so excited to have a sink with running water. However, Daddy's idea of running water was not the same as Mom's idea of running water.

Daddy fixed it so the water came up from the basement. Then the water ran out of the faucet and into a bucket in the cabinet under the sink. Of course, when the bucket would get full, someone would have to carry it out to the backyard and fling the water into the grass. But at least we had "running water."

This did eliminate some of our problems. But, it also created more problems. Now we had to be careful not to let the bucket under the sink overflow or we really had a mess.

I had to readjust my skills and learn how to check the bucket. This had to be done without creating a scene or letting one of the other kids see me looking under the sink. If they saw me opening the cabinet to check the bucket, they would yell and Mom would make me carry the bucket outside and dump it in the yard.

The Board Walk

Daddy laid four or five twelve-foot long two-by-ten planks of lumber end to end to form somewhat of a sidewalk for us to walk on to get to the driveway from the back door of our house. The area at the back door to the house was dirt and old crushed up black cinders just like the old driveway—and when it rained—well, you can imagine the mess we had.

The boards quickly became weathered and began to slightly curl up on the edges; but they sufficed as a modern day sidewalk.

Because of the planks, we constantly had splinters in our feet and stubbed toes. We were always barefoot. We didn't mind the splinters because the boards also provided hours of entertainment for us kids. If we weren't bouncing up and down on the boards in a mud hole, we were dragging them around to the front of the house and propping them up on the porch steps. This would make a very good slide—just like the one at school. We would slide down the board on a sheet of waxed paper to give us the necessary slickness to sail down and also prevent us from getting splinters in our behinds.

However, this did not work all the time. One day, I convinced our cousin Sandy to hop on the already slick board and take a fast ride! She did. Then she spent another hour or so screaming her head off! She laid across her mom's lap and was held in place by two of our aunts. They yanked her pants down around her ankles and two other aunts dug and dug trying to remove the two-inch long splinter that was imbedded in her behind!

The Sprinkler

A favorite pastime for us kids in the hot summer was to squirt each other with the garden hose. Mom bought us a yellow and white blow-up plastic wading pool and filled it with ice cold water from the garden hose. We would take turns jumping in and out of the pool while shrieking and yelling and running under the spray of water that was like a fountain spraying high over our heads. What a sight!

Of course, until we grew older, we all wore plain white cotton Sears and Roebuck underpants to swim in. Actually, plain white cotton underpants were an official uniform for the first ten years or so of our life. That's all we wore during the hot, humid summer days.

As we jumped and ran for cover from the icy water, we had to be extremely careful of four things. One, trying not to stub our toes on the boards used for the sidewalk. Two, trying not to step on our pet ducks, Nancy and Bobby, who thought they owned the yellow and white wading pool. Three, trying not to step in the gooey, smelly droppings left by our pets and the neighbor's rooster. And four, avoiding the millions of black and yellow bumblebees that swarmed over the droppings.

Saturday Night Ritual

Bath time was a Saturday night ritual. The ritual took place in the middle of the kitchen. Mom would lug the big round galvanized laundry tub up from the basement and fill it with warm water. The water was heated on the kitchen stove in big round blue and white speckled pans. Then she would carefully dump the hot water into the tub. Until we were old enough to do it ourselves, she took turns bathing each one of us and washing our hair. We all used the same water. Mom just kept warming it up.

If it was summer and real warm outside, she would carry the tub outside around the corner of the house and we would have our baths in the warm night air.

The thousands of twinkling stars and lightning bugs silently flitting around us provided an ambience to the ritual that would be etched in my mind forever.

Wash Day

Laundry was done down in the musty, dark basement with a wringer washer. After each load finished washing, Mom would strategically place each piece of clothing between the tight rollers and painstakingly turn the hand-cranked wringer to squeeze out all the excess water. Then she would empty the water left in the washing machine into a big round silver galvanized tub and drag it, with water sloshing out of it every step of the way, to the basement door and dump it down the hill. This was done at least six or seven times each wash day.

The clothes were then put in a big basket with wire handles that cut right through your fingers as it was lugged up the stairs, outside to the clothesline that ran down the hill, past the dying apple tree, and along the dirt driveway. After hanging up all the clothes, Mom would prop the clothes line up with a real long skinny pole, because invariably, one of the kids would run through the line of clothes waving their hands and arms and touching each clean piece as they went. It was usually me.

And it was usually Jerry and his friend Larry's fault. I had to run through the wash because I was dodging hard green walnuts about the size of a tennis ball. Both of the boys were perched high on the tree branch that ever so conveniently hung over the roof of Freddie. They were yanking walnuts off the tree and throwing them at me as fast as they could.

Anyway, wash day was always Monday. And Monday was a very long day. Once, just for fun, I tried to keep tally marks on the basement wall of how many trips up the stairs Mom and DeAnna made during the day. But after trying to run down and make the tally mark in between Mom and DeAnna going up and down the stairs, I realized it served no purpose. Except maybe it would have caused Mom to realize that Deanna could use some extra help. And that extra help would come from me. And I certainly did not want to get involved. So I almost rubbed the skin off my knuckles trying to make the tally marks disappear before Mom saw them.

There was one good thing about wash day. Supper was always potato soup or ham and beans and cornbread. And we always had brownies.

DeAnna and the Dishes

I cannot possibly count the number of times that I relied on the trip to the outhouse to get out of doing dishes with DeAnna. Daddy's rule was that one of us would wash dishes and the other would dry. We were the oldest, so we did the dishes.

Most evenings DeAnna would wash and I would dry. I would piddle around until she had several dishes washed ahead of my drying. She would stack them at least two feet high on the dish drainer.

I would almost rub the orange and yellow flowers off the Jewel Tea dishes taking so long to dry each one while she washed so fast. The drainer would be stacked a mile high and guess what? I had to use the bathroom.

I would dry my hands, neatly fold and lay down my dishtowel, put on my shoes and tie them real tight so I wouldn't trip on the boards walking to the outhouse. By this time, we had lovingly named the outhouse, Freddie.

Freddie

On the way out to Freddie, I would straighten the walking boards, pull a couple of straggly weeds that were peeking their heads from under the boards, and with the side of my foot scrape all the pebbles and cinders off the walking boards so the younger kids wouldn't step on them barefoot.

When I finally got to my destination, I went in, took care of business, and ran out in no time at all! No one in their right mind wanted to spend any unnecessary time in that place!

Besides, more than once, some unsuspecting visitor to Freddie laid their eyes upon an unwelcome three-foot-long pest slithering around the concrete stool or coiled up in the corner watching every move you made!

Or, just as bad, an eight-legged, black fuzzy creature with a yellow diamond on its back would quickly scurry up the wall and into one of the cracks that was already filled with cobwebs so thick that the moonlight could barely illuminate the four-foot square area.

Sauntering back to the house one night, peering into the kitchen window as I went, I could see Daddy and DeAnna standing close to each other by the kitchen sink.

DeAnna, with a bright red face, cheeks puffed out, and her teeth clamped together so tight trying hard not to cry, was yanking each dish from the drainer, half drying it, and furiously cramming it into the cabinet above her. The look on Daddy's face was not a happy one, and DeAnna was mad enough to spit nails. It looked like the dishes were almost finished though.

The next evening proved to be the end of my visiting Freddie during dish time. That night, after wasting as much time as possible during my visit, I burst through the outhouse door confident that DeAnna was finished with the dishes. I was shocked to see Daddy waiting for me. As I tried to side-step around him telling him I had to get back to help DeAnna with the dishes, he very gently took hold of my arm, cleared his throat, looked me square in my eyes, and said, "I've already taken all the dishes out of the cabinet so you can wash and dry each one by yourself tonight. And I am sure you will not have to visit Freddie during dish time again."

As I looked up into his face, the pain I suffered from seeing his disappointment in me, was worse than any physical punishment I could have received.

Paddleballs

Daddy usually took Mom to the grocery store and shopping (usually at Sears and Roebuck) every Saturday afternoon. DeAnna babysat the rest of us. Mom always brought us back a surprise when she returned from shopping. One afternoon our surprise was a little wooden paddle with a rubber ball attached to a two-foot rubber band. All of us except DeAnna got one. She was too old.

We loved those paddleballs. We played with them constantly. One afternoon, Jerry, Janie, Jacque and I were playing with ours in the dining room. The dining room had a big long dark green serving buffet with four tall legs and lots of doors and drawers. As we paddled away with our new toys, eventually, because I was the best, my rubber band got caught on the buffet leg, wrapped around it several times and SNAP! The ball broke loose from the rubber band and flew across the room, bounced against the wall, traveled across the room again, bounced off the chair and it was gone. Gone into Never Never Land— never to be found again. I THOUGHT!

As I stood leaning on the doorframe of the kitchen, I could see Jerry, Janie, and Jacque still paddling their new paddleballs, jumping, laughing, and having all sorts of contests. They would not let me have a turn with their ball, and they would not help me look for my ball.

As kids do, they became bored with the game. The three of them carefully wrapped their rubber bands around the handle of their paddles and placed them inside one of the buffet doors. They were whispering to each other as they put them away, no doubt making fun of me because I did not have one now. They did not know I could see them in the full length mirror on the basement door. I could also hear them. They were hiding their new paddle balls. FROM ME!

Later on that evening, I made a very bad mistake. I got into the buffet, took one paddleball, untied the ball, tied it onto my paddle and wrote "SUSIE" on the rubber ball with a pencil.

Third Time's a Charm

The next morning, the kids remembered the new toys and as they pulled the paddleballs out of the buffet, they were shocked to realize that Jerry's rubber ball was missing. Of course, I immediately began explaining that I had found my ball under the table after they went to bed. And trying to comfort a crying, blubbering, whining brother, I even let Jerry take turns with my paddleball after I showed him how nicely I had written my name on MY rubber ball. I explained I had written my name on my ball as soon as Mom gave them to us so we wouldn't get them mixed up. And yes, they all believed me. I was saved.

But, as the day went on, it happened again! My rubber ball got tangled up on that blasted buffet leg and POP! It was gone. Flying here and there—never to be found again. I THOUGHT!

Without mentioning a word to the kids about losing my ball again, I persuaded them to put the toys away and play something else. Again, I sneaked into the buffet, took one rubber ball off the rubber band, tied it on my paddleball, carefully wrote "SUSIE" on the rubber ball and—was in business again.

Oh my. The kids were so sad the next time they got the paddleballs out. Janie's ball was missing. We looked for her ball but didn't find it. So being the nice big sister that I was, I shared with Janie all afternoon. No one suspected a thing.

Low and behold, I had the very same accident the next day. I hit the ball; the ball went round and round the buffet leg, and ZAP! It was gone. I lost my rubber ball again! Being a pro at fixing this problem, I replaced my missing rubber ball with Jacque's and did it in no time at all. Okay, the third time's a charm. BUT…Jacque was not as easily satisfied as the other two.

It took a lot of convincing and a lot of time looking for her lost ball and explaining that I was the oldest and best at the paddleball game and that was why I still had my ball. And if explaining weren't enough, I had my very name printed on the rubber ball for everyone to see. It really was mine!

Daddy to the Rescue

Jacque didn't give up crying and carrying on about losing her precious ball. She wailed and wailed all day. And of all nights, Daddy came home early, ate supper with us, and after hearing Jacque bawl all evening made us go into the dining room again and look for her ball. And Janie's. And Jerry's. The bad part was that Daddy helped us look for them this time.

I did notice the strange looks Daddy kept giving me under his furrowed eyebrows, but I just thought he was worried about Jacque being so distraught over the lost rubber ball. We looked high and low. I kept trying to tell Daddy to never mind, I didn't mind sharing mine with them, but he insisted on helping. Well, we never found them—at least we, being Jerry, Janie, Jacque and I, never found them. We got ready for bed and that was that. I THOUGHT!

I had no longer climbed into bed and sighed a big sigh of relief when Daddy walked up to my bed, reached into his pocket, held out his hand and to my surprise had three red rubber balls lying in the palm of his huge hand—each one with "SUSIE" neatly printed on it.

All he said was "Look what I found." I was shocked and actually speechless. My mouth flew open and my eyes were wide with surprise. My first thought was: how and where? But I knew better than to ask anything as stupid as that. I knew not to say anything at all.

Of course, I started crying. Daddy very gently pulled the covers back off me, took my hand, and led me outside to the porch swing in the side yard. We sat down; he put his arm around my shoulders, and hugged me close to his side. And then we proceeded to have a long talk. We talked about lying and stealing. Actually, he talked. I listened and cried. The odd thing about the whole event was that Daddy never once raised his voice. And once again, I thought I saw such disappointment in his kind eyes that I thought he could never love anyone like me again—but I was wrong.

From Eagles to Pirates

The elementary school we attended was about two miles from our house. We rode a big rambling yellow, bus to school each day. We always took a sack lunch to school, but sometimes on Friday I was allowed to walk across the street to the drugstore for lunch. I always had the same lunch: a hamburger with pickle and mustard, a Coke, and a bag of potato chips. All this for only thirty-five cents.

Edgewood Elementary School sat on the corner of Park Road and Highway 32. It housed students in grades one through eight at one time, but changed to accommodate grades one through five as the years went by. My sisters and brother were never Edgewood Eagles at the same time. But when we were promoted to the sixth grade we moved into the newly-built school together.

What a transition we had moving from Edgewood Elementary to Madison Heights Junior and Senior High School. Several elementary schools fed into the new school, there were actually hundreds of students. There were lockers for each student. The students changed classrooms for each class. The classroom change also meant a different teacher for each subject. So many changes. My graduating class of 1962 actually ended up being the first class to start in the sixth grade and graduate from the high school.

The city of Anderson, Indiana, had three large high schools. The rivalry among the schools was remarkable. Unfortunately, after forty plus years, Madison Heights was replaced by Anderson High School. However, once a Madison Heights Pirate, always a Pirate. Madison Heights will live on in my heart forever.

Sunday

For years the whole family traveled to town to attend Sunday school and church. At first we attended a Presbyterian Church, but as time passed, we changed to the Methodist Church. When we started attending the Methodist Church, I met several new friends who went to the other schools in Anderson. So, going to church together made the transition to the new junior-senior high school a little easier. We remained friends for a long time. And we had the opportunity to spend a week at Epworth Forest Church Camp together during the summer.

After Jerry was born, because he was so ill, Mom and Daddy could not go to church with us, so Daddy would take us, drop us off and return to pick us up after the service.

I don't know how Mom managed to do it, but Sunday dinner was always in the oven when we left and ready to eat when we returned home—starving.

I especially remember the dress Mom made for me to wear on the Sunday that I was to be baptized. It was white taffeta with red polka-dots. It had a real full skirt and my crinolines made it stand out just beautifully. Mom bought me a little clear-plastic purse with red polka-dots painted on it that matched my new shiny, red, slippers.

One Sunday morning, Daddy pulled the car up in front of the church doors and all four of us girls scrambled out of the car. As we were approaching the church steps, the doors opened and people started coming out. We stopped in our tracks—wondering what was happening. We looked back to the curb for Daddy, but he had already pulled away and was headed home.

Daddy and Mom had forgotten to turn the clocks back and we were exactly an hour late to church. It was alright with us though. We walked to Grandma's house, which was only five or six blocks from the church.

Younger Brother

My younger brother, Jerry, was born in December 1946 just a few months before we moved into our new house. He was a beautiful little boy, but had some health problems. His tiny body required stomach surgery at a very early age. Mom told us that Dr. Life in New Castle, Indiana, held baby Jerry in his left hand and operated on him with his right hand when Jerry was only two weeks old. He then needed another surgery two weeks later. As Jerry grew, we teased him that the scar left by the surgery made his stomach look like it had stitches similar to those on a football.

Our whole life changed when Jerry was born. Jerry, endearingly called Jeddy and then shortened to Jed by his sisters, was special. Mom and Daddy continuously traveled back and forth to New Castle, about 30 miles one way, for doctor appointments and more surgeries.

Jerry required lots of attention. Mom was taking care of him twenty-four hours a day and I guess the remodeling of the house was put on the back burner for a few years because of all the financial and mental stress Mom and Daddy were going through. I think DeAnna and I felt like we were also put on the back burner. That was the time DeAnna became my full-time babysitter. And as the other two girls were born; she took care of them too.

I can remember when Mom and Daddy would leave the house to take Jerry to the doctor. I would press my tear-streaked, dirty face on the screen door screaming for Mom not to go. I would even make myself vomit; trying to convince her that I was sick and she should stay home with me. Mom, with her infinite wisdom, left with Daddy anyway and DeAnna would calm me down, entertain me, and eventually end up being my dearest friend.

Jerry was three years behind me in school. He was in the first grade and I was in the fourth grade the day his teacher stood at my classroom door holding his hand. His face was tear-stained, dirty, and bloody and his lower lip was swollen three times its normal size. I could hardly recognize his little misshapen face. He immediately spotted me and came running to my desk.

As I hugged him and scooted over on my bench-type desk chair, his teacher handed me a very cold, half-pint milk bottle and told me to hold it on his lip until Daddy could come and get him. He was crying uncontrollably; no doubt more scared than hurt. He had apparently had a run-in with the merry-go-round on the playground and lost.

My classmate, Larry Jordan, a boy that lived down the road from us, sat on the other side of Jerry and helped comfort the frightened little boy that ended up being his best friend until Jerry's untimely death in 1994.

Family Get-Togethers

Since we had this huge yard (or field) up on the hill behind our house, especially in the summer, all of the family gatherings were at our house. Mom had eight siblings, and each of them had a big family. It seemed like hundreds of people came and brought tons of food.

We had huge Easter egg hunts and what seemed like thousands of birthday parties. And we would have a family get together for no reason at all. My sister Janie's birthday was July 18—right in the middle of summer. It was a great reason for a family get together.

Daddy had built us a huge sandbox up on the hill behind the house. He painted it green and beige. It had a roof over it and a triangular shaped seat in each corner. Our cousins of all ages loved it. But, before we could play in the sandbox, we had to find and scoop out the stinky messes Janie's cat left for us. Then after playing in the sandbox, one of the kids would waddle down the hill with either their diaper or their white cotton underpants wet and full of sand. We spent hours upon hours in that sandbox.

And if the sandbox wasn't enough entertainment for my twenty-seven cousins, we also had a rusty, squeaky swing set with two swings and a glider. During the summer you could always find kids on the old swing set, squealing and laughing as loud as they could. Or, the youngest in our family, Jacque, would be swinging and singing, like she was in a world of her own.

When I would swing, it seemed like I could swing so high my feet would touch the light blue cloudless sky. Some days I knew that if I pumped my legs just one more time, I would surely loop right over the big pole that stretched across the top of the rusty old swing set.

Cousin Dixie

Growing up I spent a lot of time with a cousin that was only one year older than me. That cousin, Dixie Lee, and I had many, many hours of fun together.

When we were very young, Dixie loved spending time at my house. And in turn, I loved staying all night at her house. Our homes were totally opposite. She was an only child, and I think the state of confusion at our house always amazed her. She never objected to our "unique" bathroom facilities and never complained about our overcrowded sleeping arrangements.

Both of Dixie's parents worked nights so as we grew into teenagers and were deemed old enough to stay alone at her house, we spent several nights by ourselves. We would pretend to be movie stars. And most of the time we let our imaginations run wild.

At one time, she lived in a huge house. The very top floor had several bedrooms and closets that linked the rooms together. My Aunt Peggy, Dixie's mother, made apple-head dolls. She would dry apples until they were shriveled up, paint faces on them, and put the heads on stuffed, fabric bodies. These apple dolls looked so real. To me, they looked old, wrinkly, and very ugly. Aunt Peggy kept one old lady doll sitting in a rocking chair in a huge, upstairs walk-through closet. Dixie knew I was scared of the apple dolls and was always making me go into the closet. Just the sight of that old apple doll would scare the living daylights out of me!

Dixie had a pet spider monkey. His name was June Bug and he was a little pest. Dixie loved June Bug. I was petrified of him. June Bug slept with Dixie and was her constant companion—even while I was at her house.

She also had cats. We used to wrap waxed paper around the cats' hind legs with rubber bands, put the cat down on the floor, and laugh hysterically as the cats tried to walk all bound up in the waxed paper.

What's in a Name Change?

Jacque was my youngest sibling. While growing up, hardly a day went by when she wasn't dressed in her cowboy clothes, complete with gun and holster, and a long ponytail stuffed in her cowboy hat. As she grew up and her taste in fashion changed, she fancied wearing a coonskin cap. Just like Davy Crocket.

Jacque was actually the one that changed my name as we were growing up. My middle name is Sue. Mom and Daddy, aunts, uncles, cousins, and neighbors—everyone called me Susie. All the kids were fine with that. Then Jacque began talking and couldn't say "Susie." Somehow, the word "Susie" became "Terdy," which eventually was shortened to "Terd." Believe it or not, I still have nieces and nephews that call me by that dreadful nickname.

All I Want for Christmas

One year for Christmas Sue wanted Santa to bring her the famous Gerber Baby Doll. At that time, Gerber Baby Food was the number one baby food for infants. On each jar of baby food was a picture of a precious baby's chubby little angelic face. This image was used to manufacture one of the most prized baby dolls wished for by little girls everywhere. Sue wanted one. They were very expensive. Of course, Sue's parents could afford to purchase her a doll. But it was unquestionable for me to even ask for one from Santa.

Well, I begged for one anyway, and came up with a thousand reasons why I should have a Gerber Baby Doll. To my surprise, on Christmas morning under our tree laid the most beautiful doll in the world. The Gerber Baby Doll was under my Christmas tree. AND IT WAS MINE!

I remember bundling up from head to toe, traipsing through the knee-deep snow, and running down the road to Sue's house! I had to show her my Gerber Baby Doll and see what Santa had brought her and her brother, Larry. When she saw that I had gotten the doll too, she couldn't believe it! We played for hours with our rubber baby dolls that were exactly alike. We found out years later that our mothers had gotten together and ordered the dolls at the same time.

Jerry's Unmannered Pets

Unfortunately, the Gerber Baby Doll story does not end here. Jerry and Larry played together daily as Jerry grew up and his health improved. They were constantly teasing and tormenting Sue and me to the point that we would scream and fight with them. Later, we realized that this was exactly what they wanted.

Sue ended up with a puppy love crush on Jerry and that even made the teasing worse. Larry and I would chant over and over: "Sue and Jerry sitting in a tree, k i s s i n g . First came love. Then came marriage. There goes Sue pushing a baby carriage!" Oh, boy! Did they ever get teased!

One evening, after a day of teasing, Jerry and Larry decided to hide my doll. They put it in the rabbit's cage. Well, the rabbit, Big Mike, must have loved the rubber doll too, because after my searching for it for hours the next day, I found it—without any toes and fingers! Big Mike had chewed the fingers and toes off my precious Gerber Baby Doll! I was devastated!

Of course, the boys did not get into any trouble. Jerry always weaseled his way out of trouble and Mom always fell for his sob stories and let him off the hook.

Big Mike was Jerry's beautiful big, fat, white rabbit. He had Big Mike for years. The rabbit was such a pet that when we would let him out of the cage he would hop around the backyard up on the hill and finally make his way down the hill to the backdoor of our house. We actually thought Big Mike thought he was a dog. He would stand on his hind feet and scratch at the door until someone let him in and gave him just what he wanted. Usually he did not want a carrot; he wanted one of Mom's homemade chocolate brownies.

Family Pets

Jerry also had a beautiful, black Shetland pony named Tiny. We also had two other horses, Lady and Ginger. We all rode the horses and took turns feeding and taking care of them.

Everyone loved the horses except me. I did not care for them at all. I helped feed and water but did not like one minute of it and complained all the time while lugging buckets of water or feed to them.

Usually when company went to see the horses, we all went. Our friends from school were somewhat infatuated with our country living and farm atmosphere. All of us in the small horse stall plus our visitors from town made for lots of confusion and noise. This made the horses uncomfortable and nervous.

One afternoon we were all in the horse stalls. Everyone was petting and brushing the horses and feeding them sugar cubes, when Tiny got very excited! He bit Jerry on the stomach! Since we were never fully clothed, Jerry's bare tummy had a nasty bruise on it for several weeks. I thought that would be the end of Tiny for sure, but nothing happened. Daddy said it was our fault because we upset Tiny and he retaliated by biting.

Then one day, we were all up the hill behind the house playing around the horses. We were climbing on Daddy's old flatbed lumber truck pretending to be rodeo riders, jumping on the horses. I missed, fell, and broke my pelvic bone, ending up in the hospital thirty miles away.

I was really treated special by all the kids when I came home from the hospital on crutches. None of us had ever seen crutches before and were amazed at all the fun one could have swinging high up on the neat wooden sticks!

Bicycle Accident

One very hot and humid summer day, Jerry riding his shiny red and silver Schwinn bicycle and a friend, Vic, were racing their bikes through the knee-high weedy grass in the field. It looked like so much fun I just had to get in on it. So I hopped on the back of the bike, grabbed hold around Vic's waist, and stuck my legs and BARE FEET out and away we went! It seemed as though we were flying through the weeds and grass like race cars leaving the starting line.

We were soaring down the hill, screaming and yelling as the wind hit our faces and the weeds whipped our bare legs. The bicycles kept gaining momentum down the hill. Neither one of the boys heard me scream as my left foot got tangled up in the grass, weeds, and the spokes of the rear bicycle wheel.

Finally the bike stopped because of my foot, threw both of us off, and not knowing what happened, I ran all the way home on a severely mangled bloody foot. Then again, I was in the hospital and on crutches for several weeks. The other kids felt sorry for me, but sure did enjoy the chance to swing on those crutches again!

Special Birthday

On our thirteenth birthdays, Sue and I had a birthday party together—a hayride followed by a dance. We planned one together since our birthdays were only a day apart. Daddy had lights strung all around the area of the driveway that was our basketball court. We had our hi fi (high fidelity) stereo record player set up with records from all the top recorders.

Mom and Oma, Sue's mother, had fixed tons of food, and a neighbor drove the tractor that pulled the hayride wagon. It was a party never to be forgotten. Sue and I made the invitations, which was a poem that described our party.

Since she and I were only a year apart in age and went to the same school, everyone knew each other at the party. We danced, talked, laughed, and ate all evening. Sue's parents and Mom and Daddy walked around and visited with all the kids.

Of course, we had a couple of boys from another high school try to "crash" the party. They were not invited and arriving uninvited was just unheard of in those days. Daddy very politely escorted the boys down our steep driveway and headed them toward town. The boys had walked out to the house from town, so now they had a long, dark, quiet walk home.

Daddy's Little Girl

My younger sister Janie, or Juanita Jane, was named for Daddy's mother. She was actually Daddy's first-born girl since DeAnna and I were his step-daughters.

She was also my cute little skinny, persnickety sister. She was always tattling on one of us. Janie was the cause of me getting my mouth washed out with a bar of orange colored Lifeboy soap more than once. If I called her "cootie-bug" once, I called her "cootie-bug" a thousand times. She hated it; so I persevered. Actually, I don't even know where the silly name came from. Janie was so tiny and cute and Mom kept her hair curled in little tiny pin curls that framed her miniature face. But she tattled. I did the name calling. And Mom punished me by grinding the horrible tasting orange soap into my teeth.

Janie was always at the wrong place at the wrong time. If any one of us got our fingers smashed under the walk boards—it was Janie. If any one of us got stung by a bee—it was Janie. If anyone stepped on a rusty old nail—it was Janie. When Mrs. Schmidt's porch swing broke, it was Janie that got her skinny little leg caught under it.

Janie loved cats. She had one special cat that she particularly loved. She used to work patiently on Mom's treasured Singer treadle sewing machine making clothes for her ugly cat. She then proceeded to dress the cat and push him around the house in her doll buggy. Of course, that usually led to more name calling by me, more screaming by Janie, and more Lifeboy Soap.

Janie had the shrillest, high-pitched voice of any child I'd ever heard in my entire life. I can remember secretly praying before she went to the hospital to have her tonsils removed, that removing the tonsils would change the squeaky pitch of her voice. The tonsillectomy did not change a thing.

Our Neighbors

We were lucky enough not to have any neighbors to the east of us. Our only neighbors were to the west.

There were no houses across the road from our house until the late fifties when they actually moved a whole house from the city. We watched in awe as the big house just seemed to pop up like a mushroom right in the middle of the field.

In the house right next door to us, Mrs. Schmidt raised five kids all by herself. I didn't know if she was a widow or a divorcee. I just knew there was not a Mr. Schmidt.

I loved Mrs. Schmidt. She was a short, petite lady that always wore dresses and nylons with black seams up the back of her legs.

If I looked real closely when she was swinging on her porch swing, which was one of her favorite things, I could see the elastic garters that tightly secured her nylon hose right below her knees. The garters looked like they could stop the blood flow to her legs at any given minute. I know now that Mrs. Schmidt would have been so embarrassed if she ever knew I could see her garters beneath her lacy white slip that usually was hanging out from her dress.

She was so pretty. She always had a perfectly round circle of pink rouge painted on each cheek, and wore a beautiful strand of big round soft, pale pink beads. The beads hung elegantly above her ample bosom.

She loved to talk. Mom used to say Mrs. Schmidt could talk your arm off, but she would do anything for our family and was a wonderful neighbor.

All five of Mrs. Schmidt's kids were older than me. But I have several fond memories of each of them. Gerald, Clyde, Jack, Lola, and Joan were all hard working, good kids.

Lola's daughter, Patty, spent a lot of time at her grandma's house. And when she came to her grandma's house she ran right over to our house. She loved to come over and became best friends with Janie. They played together every time Patty visited.

Patty always wanted to be our sister and to this day, we think of her as just that—our sister-wannabe.

Mrs. Schmidt loved to pick blackberries. During June, usually on what seemed to be the hottest day of summer, I could always count on her asking Mom and me to go with her back to the berry patches behind her house. I remember her looking so out of character in her "berry pickin' clothes." She would wear a long sleeved, plaid, flannel men's shirt, jeans, thick socks, and brown boots that laced. She would still have her pink rouge in perfect little circles on each cheek and that just made her pretty blue eyes sparkle and dance underneath her big brimmed straw hat.

As we were trudging through the knee-high grass and thistles and into the thickets of the berry patch, we were prodding and poking a few steps ahead with a stick to scare away the snakes.

I would be the leader. Mom was always right behind me. And Mrs. Schmidt would be last in line, swinging her big dented berry pickin' pan and talking a mile a minute.

S. D. J.

As you head down the hill West from Mrs. Schmidt's house, past her cherry and apple trees and through the yard that belonged to the Cook family, you'll find Pudgy, an English bulldog tied to his doghouse. He belongs to the Jordan family.

In front of Pudgy's doghouse was a big white two story house. It belonged to Oma and Bob Jordan and their four children—Bob, Ronnie, Larry, and Susan. I spent countless number of days and nights at the Jordan's.

Susan (Sue) was the youngest of the four children. She was and still is my very best friend. Sue and I had so many things in common.

For instance, her initials were S.D.J. and my initials were D. S. J. Her birthday was October 4 and my birthday was October 3. She had three brothers and I had three sisters. We were one year apart in age. Sue contracted polio when we were young. The doctors thought I had polio when I was young. There were so many likenesses between the two of us.

We knew we were destined to be best friends for life. And we are.

Warm Snickerdoodles

Sue and I were like sisters. We shared clothes, books, and toys. I loved going to her house.

Sue's mother was always eager to play some kind of a trick on us. At night, she would try to scare us to death as we walked back and forth from their house to ours. She used to stoop down almost crawling on her hands and knees to hide in the tall weeds that lined the road in front of Mrs. Schmidt's house and Cook's house. She would make weird, scary sounds as she jumped out and grabbed us. Even though we sort of expected her to be hiding somewhere along our path, we still screamed at the top of our lungs as we grabbed each other's hands and ran as fast as we could.

And we could never be sure, when we climbed into bed at night, if she was hiding under the blankets at the foot of the bed ready to grab our feet. She always laughed warmheartedly as we screamed our heads off while hugging each other and spinning around as if it were the end of the world.

Mrs. Jordan always apologized for scaring us and made us feel better by giving us a couple of big, round, cinnamon snickerdoodle cookies that she had baked that afternoon.

After she was diagnosed with polio, Sue had to make several trips back and forth to Indianapolis for surgery on her legs. She was in a plaster body cast and leg casts for months at a time. I did not realize until years later how much I admired her for her being so brave during those uncomfortable and painful days. I traveled with the family to take her to Riley Children's Hospital in Indianapolis. We were inseparable for days on end.

A Home Built by Love

Today, driving out of town, headed west on Eighth Street Road, I wind around the beautiful tree-lined road that houses many luxurious homes.

I turn onto the beautiful cement driveway that winds up the hill leading to the house of my childhood. Parking the car in front of a double car garage, I make a mental note that the sandbox is missing; the swing set is no longer on top of the hill; and Freddie is not standing beside the driveway. Even the old walnut tree that stood guarding him has been removed.

Instead, the well manicured grass and beautiful flowers nod their heads as a cool breeze gently awakens my senses and nudges me back to reality.

Jacque and her husband live there and have since Daddy passed away in 1975 and Mom moved on with her life. They have made several very nice visible improvements throughout the years. It is very evident that this house and surrounding yard is very much loved.

The attic of the house caught fire in December 2006, forcing them to make some drastic changes on the house itself. The house went through some major cosmetic changes, but Jacque was adamant about keeping some of Daddy's beautiful workmanship in as many places as possible.

This house has many wonderful and unique childhood memories and secrets neatly tucked into each corner and hidden under the concrete amidst the dirt and dust in the old basement floor.

Indeed, the old homestead has been transformed into a beautiful house. But the sentimental memories of growing up there will never be erased from my mind. The house is truly a home built by love.

Reminiscing

As I pause and take a few minutes to reminisce about my early childhood days through the eyes of an adult, I realize that my life was dramatically influenced by Mom and Daddy.

Although Daddy was a man of few words, those words were so powerful and his actions were so life altering. Daddy was so kind and considerate of everyone. He touched the hearts of so many people in his life. And I don't think he realized what an impression he made on his children—especially me.

The lessons we learned from Mom, even though our lives were drastically different from hers as we raised our children, were lessons that only a mother can convey to her offspring.

The old saying, "actions speak louder than words" was surely written as a tribute to my Mom and Daddy. They showered all of their children with much more love than they could ever show on the surface.

In a family with her children, his children, and their children, the love was never divided—always equal to all of us—always enough to go around. And for that and all of the beautiful, everlasting memories and impressions my parents created for me I am so thankful. I only hope and pray that I made such life altering impressions and memories for my children like Mom and Daddy made for me.